W9-AKD-614

Great African Americans

# MARY CHURCH TERRELL

## LeaDeR foR equaLity

Revised Edition

**Patricia and Fredrick McKissack**

**Enslow Publishers, Inc.**

40 Industrial Road       PO Box 38
Box 398       Aldershot
Berkeley Heights, NJ 07922    Hants GU12 6BP
USA       UK

http://www.enslow.com

*To Ching, Bob, and Mary*

Revised edition of *Mary Church Terrell: Leader for Equality* © 1991

**Library of Congress Cataloging–in–Publication Data**

McKissack, Pat, 1944–
    Mary Church Terrell : leader for equality / Patricia and Fredrick
McKissack. — Rev. ed.
        p. cm. — (Great African Americans)
    Includes index.
    ISBN 0-7660-1697-8
    1. Terrell, Mary Church, 1863–1954 — Juvenile literature. 2. African American women — Biography — Juvenile literature. 3. African Americans — Biography — Juvenile literature. 4. Civil rights workers — United States — Biography — Juvenile literature. 5. African American women social reformers — Biography — Juvenile literature. 6. African Americans — Segregation — History — Juvenile literature. 7. African Americans — Civil rights — History — Juvenile literature. [1. Terrell, Mary Church, 1863–1954. 2. Civil rights workers. 3. African Americans — Biography. 4. Women — Biography.] I. McKissack, Fredrick. II. Title. III. Series.
    E185.97.T47 M35   2001
    323'.092 — dc21
                                    00-012416

Printed in the United States of America

10 9 8 7 6 5 4 3 2 1

**To Our Readers**
We have done our best to make sure all Internet addresses in this book were active and appropriate when we went to press. However, the author and the publisher have no control over and assume no liability for the material available on those Internet sites or on other Web sites they may link to. Any comments or suggestions can be sent by e — mail to comments@enslow.com or to the address on the back cover.

Every effort has been made to locate all copyright holders of material used in this book.
If any errors or omissions have occurred, corrections will be made in future editions of this book.

**Illustration Credits:** © Corel Corporation, p. 6; Courtesy of the National Register of Historic Places, p. 13B; U.S. Department of Defense, p. 18; Library of Congress, pp. 7, 19, 20, 23, 25; Moorland-Spingarn Research Center, Howard University, pp. 4, 9, 15, 16T, 16B, 22, 24, 26; National Archives, p. 13T; Photographs and Prints Division, Schomburg Center for Research in Black Culture, The New York Public Library, Astor, Lenox and Tilden Foundations, p. 30; Oberlin College Archives, Oberlin, Ohio, pp. 3, 10, 11, 27; Reproduced from *Old Washington, D.C. in Early Photographs, 1846–1932*, published by Dover Publications, Inc., 1980, p. 12.

**Cover Credits:** Library of Congress; Moorland-Spingarn Research Center, Howard University; Oberlin College Archives, Oberlin, Ohio.

# TABLE OF CONTENTS

# Mary Church Terrell
## September 23, 1863–July 24, 1954

CHAPTER 1

# The Best of Everything

I t was 1863. Mary Eliza Church was born in Memphis, Tennessee. Her parents were Robert and Louisa Church.

Robert Church had been born a slave. Mary was born free! Robert wanted his wife and daughter to have the best of everything.

Robert bought and sold land. Soon he was a very rich man. Mary grew up in a grand old house with big rooms. Her special place was in the flower garden. She enjoyed learning the flowers' names.

**As a little girl, Mary loved learning the names of flowers.**

In the 1870s unfair laws were being passed. Black people were losing their rights. And the laws didn't help them.

Louisa and Robert separated. Louisa started her own business. Both of Mary's parents had money. And they loved Mary. But it was not enough to keep the unfair laws in the South from hurting her.

What could they do? At last Robert and Louisa decided to send Mary to Ohio. They would miss her. But in the North she could go to a good school. She would be safe.

Mary's parents sent her north to a better school in Ohio. This photo shows Cleveland, Ohio, in the early 1900s.

7

CHAPTER 2

# Wild Ideas!

t he years passed quickly. Mary grew into a beautiful young woman. She was also smart. She was well liked by her teachers and friends.

Mary graduated at the top of her class in 1879. Many of her friends married after high school. But not Mary Eliza Church. She wanted to go to college.

Some people thought that was a wild idea. At that time, not many women went to college — especially not black women.

**Mary was always very interested in women's rights.**

**Mary studied hard at Oberlin College.**

Oberlin College in Ohio was different from most schools in the 1880s. Men, women, and African Americans went to school together. Lots of people thought that was a wild idea, too. They thought there should be separate schools for men, for women, and for African Americans.

Mary enjoyed learning about the past and the present. Oberlin was full of new ideas. *Women should have the right to vote!*

Now that was really a wild idea! Mary didn't think so.

In 1884 Mary finished her studies at Oberlin. Her father sent her to Europe in 1888. Mary decided to live there for a while. She studied music and great writings.

In 1890 Mary came back to the United States. She had so many job choices.

**Mary was one of the first black women to earn a college degree.**

11

**Mary moved to Washington, D.C., to teach school.**

Come work at Oberlin! Come teach in Alabama! No, come to New York!

In college, Mary began a friendship with Frederick Douglass, the famous civil rights leader.

Mary had met a young teacher named Robert Heberton Terrell. He lived in Washington, D.C. Come marry me, he asked. And she answered yes.

Mrs. Mary Church Terrell was a very beautiful bride. She also worked for equal rights for African Americans and women. Some people thought that was a wild idea. But not Mrs. Terrell.

The Mary Church Terrell House still stands at 326 'T' Street N.W. in Washington, D.C.

13

CHAPTER 3

# Women of Color

In the 1890s, neither black nor white women had many rights. They couldn't vote. They couldn't hold public office. They couldn't go to some schools or work at some jobs. And segregation stopped the races from working or living together.

Mrs. Terrell wrote to a friend in 1894: "There should not be segregation in the nation's capital." What could one woman of color do? Plenty!

In 1895 Mrs. Terrell was asked to serve on the

Washington, D.C., school board. She worked to make the schools better.

One law she wanted to pass said that all children—boys and girls—had to go to school until age fourteen.

Mrs. Terrell cared about education. She was the first black woman in the United States to serve on a school board.

Mary married Robert Heberton Terrell, above. Their daughter, Phyllis, left, was born in 1898.

The men on the school board laughed at her idea. The law didn't pass. But Mary wouldn't give up. She never stopped working for better schools.

Mrs. Terrell met other women of color who were working for equal rights, too. In 1896 all the African-American women's groups joined under one name: the National Association of Colored Women. Mary Church Terrell was the first president. She served from 1896 to 1901.

President Theodore Roosevelt named Robert Terrell a judge. He was the first black man to be chosen as a judge in the country's capital.

16

CHAPTER 4

# It Isn't Fair!

t he National Association for the Advancement of Colored People (NAACP) was started in 1909. Mary joined soon after. Men, women, blacks, and whites worked together for the rights of all Americans.

Mrs. Terrell also helped start groups for young college women. Women still belong to these groups today.

In World War I, black soldiers fought in separate units. They were not allowed to fight

**In World War I, black soldiers helped the United States fight for freedom. But they were kept separate from the white soldiers.**

alongside white soldiers. Mary spoke out. *It isn't fair!* she said.

The war ended. Black soldiers came home. They had been fighting for freedom in Europe. But they didn't have freedom at home. Mary spoke out again. *It isn't fair!* she said.

The world had fought a war for freedom. But women still couldn't vote. Mary spoke out once more. *It isn't fair!* she said.

18

**Mary also believed that women should be allowed to vote.**

**This poster invited people to join the NAACP. The group was started to work for the rights of Americans of all races.**

Mary and other women like her spoke out for rights and freedom. Would things ever get better?

Then, in 1920, the law was changed. At last women had the right to vote. Things were getting better. But not for African Americans.

Women could vote. But black women who lived in the South couldn't vote. Neither could black men.

Mary wrote: "I could vote. But many other women of color could not vote. . . ." *It isn't fair!* she said.

CHAPTER 5

# "It Took Long Enough!"

ary Church Terrell spoke all over the world. Once, when she was in Europe, she gave her speech in three languages: English, German, and French. People were surprised.

In 1940 she wrote her own life story, *A Colored Woman in a White World*. "I am no better off than the poorest woman of my race," she said. She spent the rest of her life working for the rights of all people.

21

**In 1904 Mary Terrell spoke at the International Congress of Women in Berlin, Germany. She talked about freedom and equality.**

By 1953 her husband, Judge Terrell, had died. Mrs. Terrell was eighty-nine years old. And Washington, D.C., was still a segregated city.

Mrs. Terrell and a group of other blacks went to some segregated restaurants. They quietly took seats. And each time, they were asked to leave.

The NAACP helped Mrs. Terrell's group. They took the case to the Supreme Court, the highest court in the United States. But the judge ruled that the restaurants could stay segregated. They did not have to serve African Americans.

*It isn't fair!* said Mary whenever she saw signs separating white and black people.

Mrs. Terrell had light skin. Sometimes people thought she was white, and they were nicer to her. She always told the truth. She wanted to teach people that it was wrong to judge others by the color of their skin.

Still, the case helped make people think more about the problem. Soon some places in Washington chose to end segregation. A law was finally passed ending all segregation in the nation's capital.

**Mrs. Terrell wished for a world where blacks and whites could eat at the same lunch counter.**

Even when she was very old, Mrs. Terrell, second from left,
still worked for equal rights. Above, she
protested against whites-only restaurants in Washington, D.C.

Mrs. Terrell was old and very sick. She didn't have long to live. In 1954 the NAACP took another case to the highest court. This time, the judges ruled that schools should not be segregated.

Friends told Mrs. Terrell the good news. She had worked all her life for equal rights. "It took long enough," she said, smiling. Just two months later she died in Annapolis, Maryland.

**All through her life, Mary Church Terrell spoke out for rights and freedom.**

# timeline

1863 ~ Born on September 23 in Memphis, Tennessee.

1879 ~ Graduates from high school in Ohio; enters Oberlin College.

1884 ~ Graduates from Oberlin College.

1885 ~ Begins career as a teacher.

1888 ~ Earns master's degree from Oberlin; begins traveling and studying in Europe.

1884

1890 ~ Returns to the United States.

1891 ~ Marries Robert Heberton Terrell.

1896 ~ Becomes the first president of the National Association of Colored Women.

1904 ~ Gives a famous speech at the International Congress of Women in Berlin, Germany.

1940 ~ Publishes her life story, *A Colored Woman in a White World*.

1954 ~ Dies in Annapolis, Maryland, on July 24.

1891

# WORDS to KNOW

**graduate** — To finish all the studies at a school.

**judge** — The person who decides a court case.

**National Association for the Advancement of Colored People (NAACP)** — An organization started to help all Americans gain equal rights and protection under the law.

**National Association of Colored Women** — An organization that included all African-American women's groups.

**Oberlin College** — A college in Ohio that was not segregated in the early 1800s. At that time, most colleges were for white students only.

**president** — The leader of a country or group.

**public office** — A position of service to citizens of a city, state, or country.

**school board** — A group of people who manage the way the schools in the area will be run.

# Words to Know

**segregation** — The separation of people based on race, religion, age, sex, or some other reason.

**slave** — A person who is owned by another. That person can be bought or sold.

**Supreme Court** — The highest court in the country.

**Washington, D.C.** — The city where the United States government is located. D.C. stands for District of Columbia.

Segregation laws kept people apart. Blacks could not sit near whites at movie theaters.

# LEARN MORE about MARY CHURCH TERRELL

## Books

Beckner, Chrisanne. *100 African-Americans Who Shaped American History*. San Mateo, Calif.: Bluewood Books, 1995.

Swain, Gwenyth. *Civil Rights Pioneer: A Story About Mary Church Terrell*. Minneapolis, Minn.: Lerner Publishing Group, 1999.

## Internet Addresses

*About.com Black History*
Biography, photos, and links to other history makers and Web sites.
   **<http://terrysarge.homestead.com/marychurchterrell. html>**

*Library of Congress, America's Story from America's Library*
A short biography and photos.
   **<http://www.americaslibrary.gov/pages/jb_0923_ terrell_1.html>**

# index